DOMINICK ARGENTO

SEASONS

for SATB Chorus a cappella

Text by Pat Solstad

Published by Boosey & Hawkes, Inc.
229 West 28st Street
New York NY 10001

www.boosey.com

AN IMAGEM COMPANY

© Copyright 2012 by Boosey & Hawkes, Inc.
International Copyright Secured.
All Rights Reserved.

ISMN 979-0-051-48191-0

First printed 2012
Second printing 2013
Printed and distributed by Hal Leonard Corporation, Milwaukee WI
Seasons © Copyright 2012 by Pat Solstad

SEASONS

I. Autumn

Cool, misty mornings now bathe parched lawns,
yet there's a teasing as temperatures occasionally climb.
Persistent Summer is struggling to upstage the next performer.

But it is Autumn's turn.
Enrobed in blazing reds and golds,
she cries out, announcing herself with drunken joy,
knowing it's her time to be adored.

Short-lived, the raucous voice slowly transforms into a moan.
As she stands alone, stripped of her once-stunning beauty,
Winter arrives. With comforting arms, he gathers her up
and covers her with his soothing blanket of silver-white.

Humming an ancient lullaby, he rocks her to sleep
and she drifts into dreams of her glory days.
Certain they will come again in time she smiles, sighs, and
slowly slips away.

II. Winter

Master Artist Winter draws his hand across the landscape and
snowflakes appear. He guides them as they cover bare trees,
picnic tables, and abandoned farm machinery,
creating elegant monochromatic sculptures.

Without warning, his mood
changes from serene to stormy.
He shakes his fist, stomps his feet,
and howls with intense fury.

His rage increases as he rips limbs
from trembling trees and flings garbage cans around,
sending them banging and clanging into empty streets.
All creatures cower.

Children peer impatiently from windows,
rabbits flee to cool warrens, and birds
sink deeper into the sanctuary
of their soft nests.

Winter, now lacking an audience, blusters a bit more,
a reminder that he is still in charge.
Then, anger spent, he becomes the Master Artist once again.
With a stroke of his paintbrush, skies clear to a placid
blue, his preparation for
the delightful intrusion of the regal red cardinal.

III. Spring

With sweet baby breath, Spring blows away Winter's crumbling canvas.
He calls to the soft rains to bathe him.
The gentle breezes dry him and
the sun smiles as it warms his naked newness.

He commands hyacinth and crocus to appear
and nudges sleepy buttercups.
He welcomes the arrival of the handsome coyote pups,
as their joyful parade passes by.

Delighted children burst into the open,
like wild colts too long confined,
and run screaming through yards, dodging flailing sheets
on newly hung clotheslines.

Then Spring, feeling quite smug,
slips into his royal robe,
struts about, surveying his kingdom,
and grins.

IV. Summer

Out of the mists of Spring,
the Goddess of Summer arrives,
arms outstretched, eager
to perform her annual miracle.

Joyful acolytes shed their leafy bedclothes.
Ferns unfurl, coral bells awaken, roses lift their faces
to the golden sun, and lilacs
fill the air with intoxicating perfume.

Fireflies flicker in night skies, in concert
with moonlight and shooting stars.
Bathed in this celestial light,
fragrant angel's trumpets reflect a ghostly glow.

Soon, the Goddess of Summer sees
that all is proceeding as planned.
Though reluctant to leave, she nods
and sadly bestows her loving benediction.

–Pat Solstad

for Dale Warland
with admiration and affection
PS & DA

PAT SOLSTAD

SEASONS

DOMINICK ARGENTO

for mixed chorus a cappella

I. Autumn

Copyright © 2012 by Boosey & Hawkes, Inc.
International Copyright Secured. All rights reserved.
Seasons, Copyright © 2012 by Pat Solstad.

979-0-051-48191-0

979-0-051-48191-0

979-0-051-48191-0

trattenuto
poco a poco crescendo
19
out, an-nounc-ing her - self with drunk-en joy, know -
poco a poco crescendo
out, an-nounc-ing her - self with drunk-en joy, know -
poco a poco crescendo
out, an-nounc-ing her - self with drunk-en joy, know -
poco a poco crescendo
out, an-nounc-ing her - self with drunk-en joy, know -
trattenuto
poco a poco crescendo
ff
f

poco rall.
rall.
22
- ing it's her time to be a - dored. Short -
- ing it's her time to be a - dored. Short -
- ing it's her time to be a - dored. Short -
- ing it's her time to be a - dored. Short -
poco rall.
rall.

Più mosso (♩= 76 ca.)
25
mf
mp
rall.
-lived, her rau - cous voice slow - ly trans - forms in - to a moan.
-lived, her rau - cous voice slow - ly trans - forms in - to a moan.
-lived, her rau - cous voice slow - ly trans - forms in - to a moan.
-lived, her rau - cous voice slow - ly trans - forms in - to a moan.
Più mosso (♩= 76 ca.)
rall.
a tempo
allargando
29
p
poco a poco crescendo
As she stands a - lone, stripped of her once - stun - ning
As she stands a - lone, stripped of her once - stun - ning
As she stands a - lone, stripped of her once - stun - ning
As she stands a - lone, stripped of her once - stun - ning
a tempo
allargando
p
poco a poco crescendo

a tempo

33

ten. *f sub. p*

beau - ty, Win - ter ar - rives. Win - ter ar - rives.

ten. *f sub. p*

beau - ty, Win - ter ar - rives. Win - ter ar - rives.

ten. *f* *p*

beau - ty, Win - ter ar - rives, ar - rives.

ten. *f sub. p*

beau - ty, Win - ter ar - rives. Win - ter ar - rives.

a tempo

ten.

ten. *f* *sub. p*

979-0-051-48191-0

51
He rocks her to sleep and she drifts,
He rocks her to sleep and she drifts,
He rocks her to sleep and she drifts,
(humming)

57
drifts in - to dreams of her glo - ry days. And
drifts in - to dreams of her glo - ry days. And
drifts in - to dreams of her glo - ry days. And
(humming)
...her glo - ry days. And

Tempo Io (♩ = 67 ca.)
63
rall.
Cer-tain they will come a-gain in time she smiles, sighs and
Cer-tain they will come a-gain in time she smiles, sighs and
Cer-tain they will come a-gain in time she smiles, sighs and
Cer-tain they will come a-gain in time she smiles, and... (humming
Tempo Io (♩ = 67 ca.)
rall.
Come prima (♩. = 53 ca.)
dim. e rall.
69
pp
slow - ly slips a - way.
slow - ly slips a - way.
slow - ly slips a - way.
Come prima (♩. = 53 ca.)
dim. e rall.
pp

II. Winter

979-0-051-48191-0

9
mp
mf
pic - nic ta - bles, and a - ban - doned farm ma-chin-er-y,
11
meno f
cre - at - ing mon - o-chro-mat - ic sculp-tures

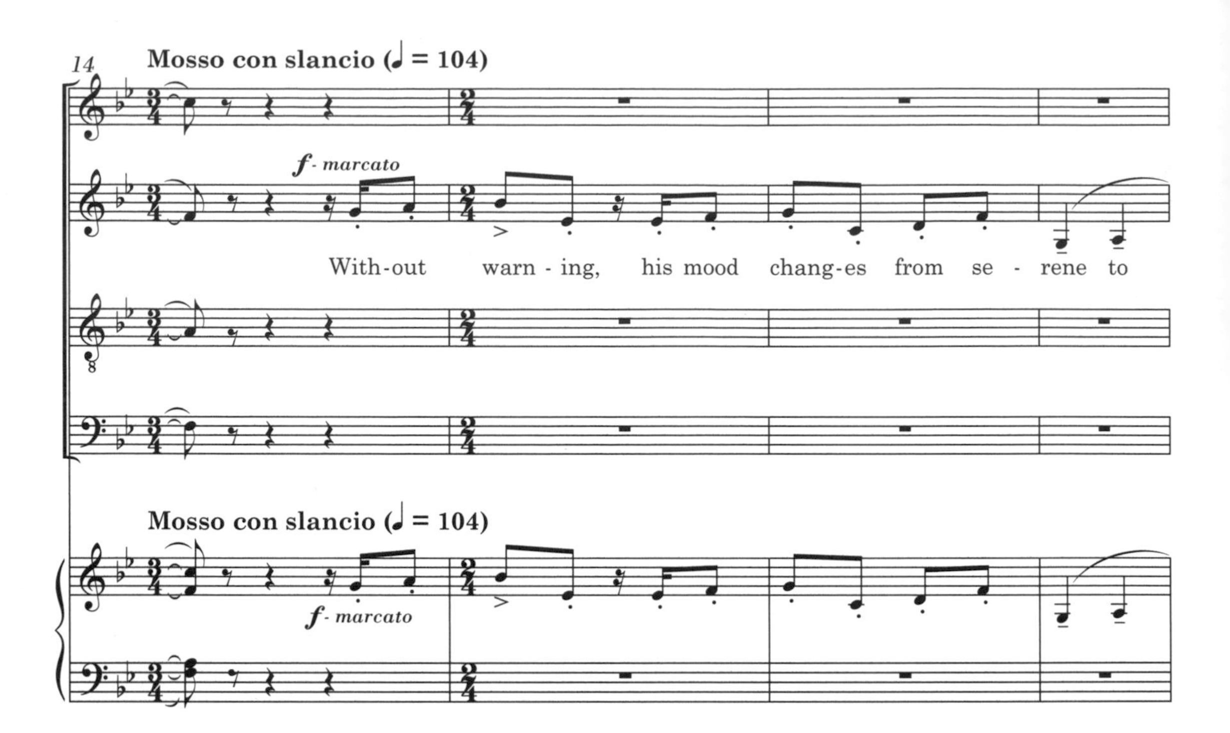
14
Mosso con slancio (♩ = 104)
f - marcato
With-out warn - ing, his mood chang-es from se - rene to
Mosso con slancio (♩ = 104)
f - marcato

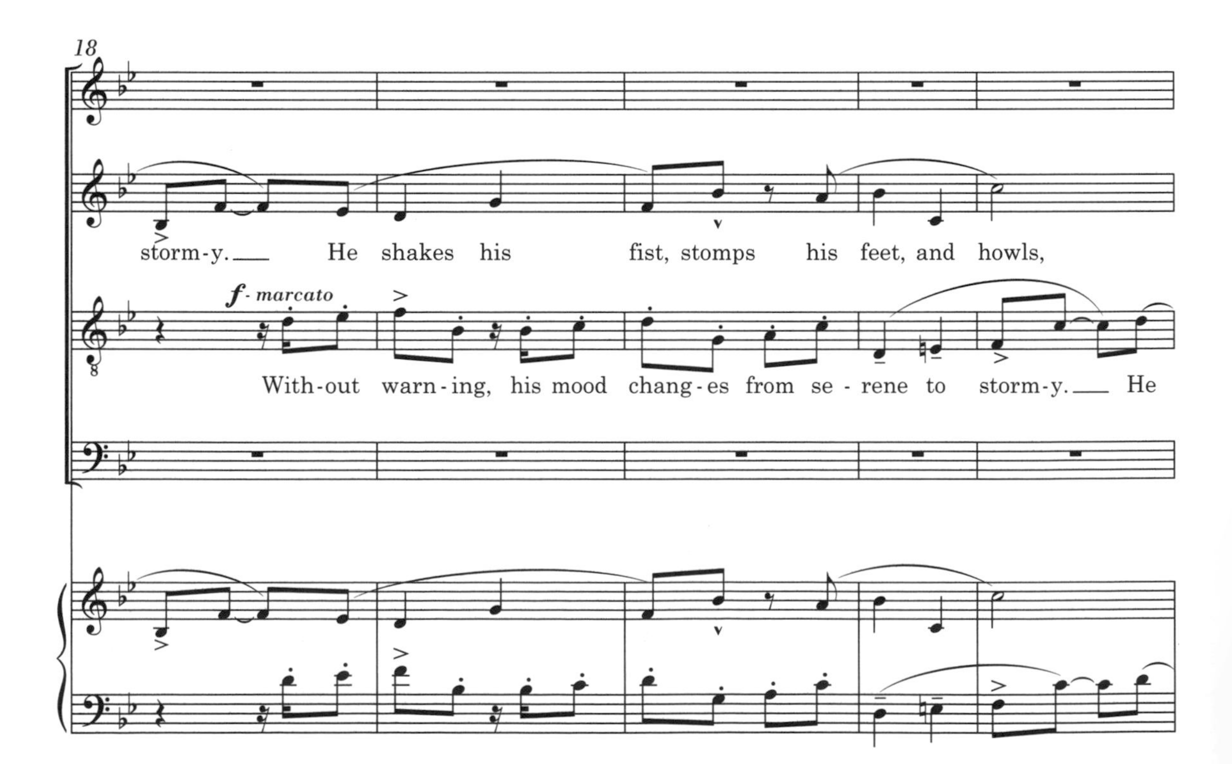
18
storm-y. He shakes his fist, stomps his feet, and howls,
f - marcato
With-out warn-ing, his mood chang-es from se - rene to storm-y. He

23
with in - tense
fu - ry.
He stomps his feet and he
shakes his fist, stomps his feet, shakes his fist and stomps his feet.
f - marcato
With-out
f
28
f - marcato
With - out
howls. His rage in - creas-es as he rips limbs from
Shakes his fist, stomps his feet and howls,
warn - ing. his mood chang - es from se - rene to storm-y. He

32

warn - ing, his mood chang - es from se - rene to storm - y. ___ He

trem - bling trees and flings ___ gar - bage cans a - round,

___ His rage in - creas - es as he rips limbs ___ from

shakes his fist, stomps his feet, and howls. ___

36

shakes his fist, stomps his feet, and howls. ___

send - ing them bang - ing ___ and clang - ing in - to emp - ty

trem - bling trees and flings ___ gar - bage cans a - round,

___ His rage in - creas - es as he rips limbs ___ from

cresc.

40
ff -strepitoso
His rage in - creas - es as he rips limbs from
streets. - All crea - tures cow - er as he rips limbs
send - ing them bang - ing and clang - ing in - to emp - ty streets..
trem - bling trees, flings gar - bage cans a-round,
3

44
trem - bling trees, flings gar - bage...
from the trem - bling trees.
All crea - tures cow - er.
send - ing them bang - ing and clang - ing.

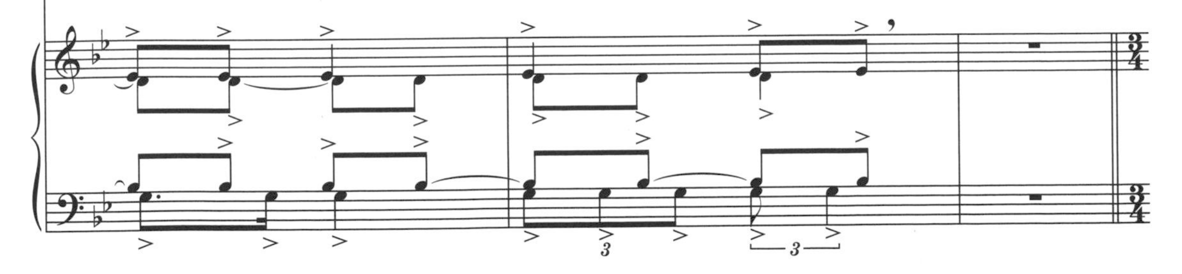

Lo stesso tempo
47
p
mf
Chil-dren peer im - pa-tient-ly from win-dows, rab-bits flee to
Lo stesso tempo
52
f
cool war-rens, and birds sink deep-er in-to the sanc-tu-ar-y

57
mp
of their soft nests.
of their soft nests.
of their soft nests.
of their soft nests.
mp

Meno mosso (♩ = 92 ca.)
61
mf
Win - ter, now lack - ing an au - di-ence, blus-ters a
Win - ter, now lack - ing an au - di-ence, blus-ters a
Win - ter, now lack - ing an au - di-ence, blus-ters a
Win - ter, now lack - ing an au - di-ence, blus-ters a
Meno mosso (♩ = 92 ca.)
mf

65
ff
bit more, a re - mind-er that he is still in charge. Then,
bit more, a re - mind-er that he is still in charge. Then,
bit more, a re - mind - er that he is still in charge. Then,
bit more, a re - mind-er that he is still in charge. Then,
ff
71
mf
molto cresc.
allarg.
an - ger spent, he be - comes the
an - ger spent, he be - comes the
an - ger spent, he be - comes
an - ger spent, he be - comes the
allarg.
molto cresc.

979-0-051-48191-0

81
(mf)
— for the de - light - ful in - tru - sion
— for the de - light - ful in - tru - sion
— for the de - light - ful in - tru - sion
— for the de - light - ful in - tru - sion
rall.
84
(f) ten.
ff
of the re - gal red car - di - nal.
of the re - gal red car - di - nal.
of the re - gal red car - di - nal.
of the re - gal red car - di - nal.
rall.
ten.

III. Spring

Maestoso con moto (𝅗𝅥 = 70)
SOPRANO
ALTO
TENOR
BASS
f
With sweet ba-by breath, Spring blows a-way win-ter's
Maestoso con moto (𝅗𝅥 = 70)
PIANO
(for rehearsal only)
6
mf
crum-bling can-vas. He calls to the soft rains to bathe him.
mp dolce

11
mf
The gen - tle breez - es dry him, and the
The gen - tle breez - es dry him, and the
The gen - tle breez - es dry him, and the
The gen - tle breez - es dry him, and the

15
sun smiles as it warms his na - ked new - ness.
sun smiles as it warms his na - ked new - ness.
sun smiles as it warms his na - ked new - ness.
sun smiles as it warms his na - ked new - ness.

20
f
p
He com-mands hy-a-cinth and cro-cus to ap-pear, and nudg-es sleep-y but-ter-cups.
27
mf
f – maestoso
He wel-comes the ar-ri-val of hand-some coy-

33
-o-te pups, as their joy-ful pa-rade passes
-o-te pups, as their joy-ful pa-rade passes
-o-te pups, as their joy-ful pa-rade passes
-o-te pups, as their joy-ful pa-rade passes

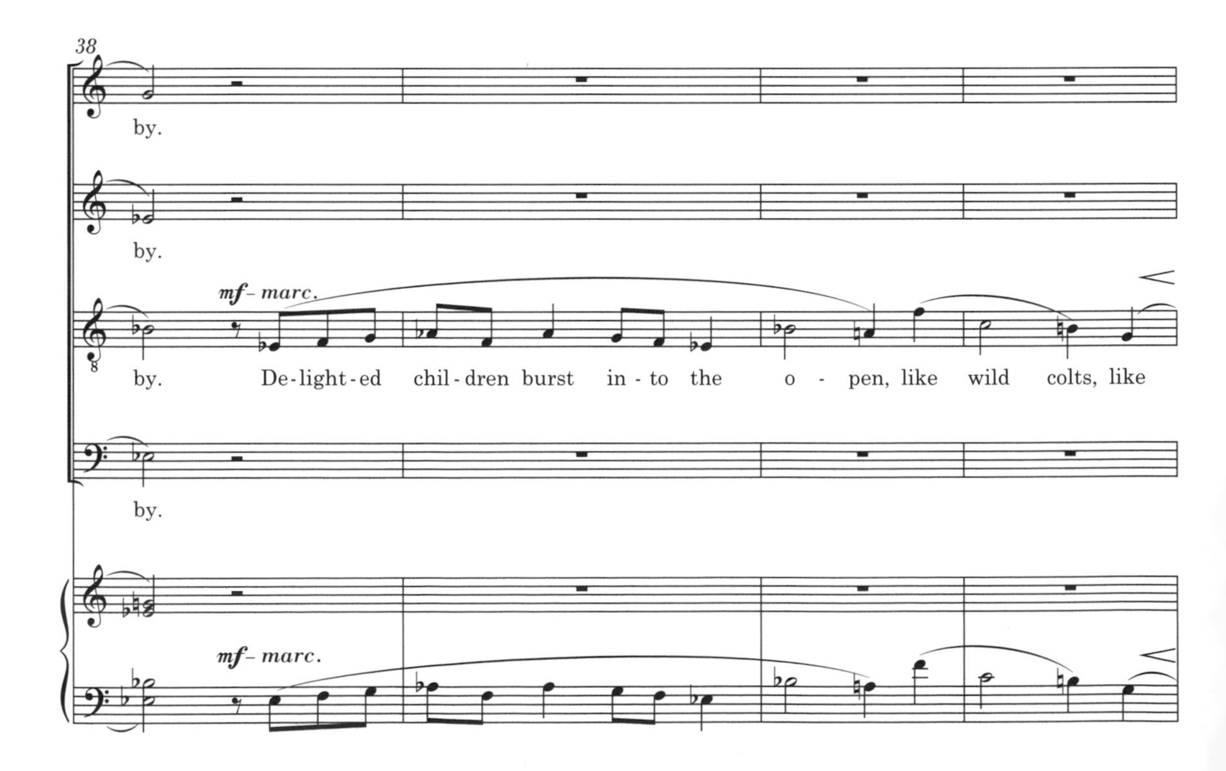
38
by.
by.
mf – marc.
by. De-light-ed chil-dren burst in-to the o-pen, like wild colts, like
by.
mf – marc.

42
mf – marc.
De-light-ed chil-dren burst in-to the o - pen, like
f
mf
wild colts too long con-fined, and run scream-ing through yards, run
f
mf – marc.
46
f
mf
wild colts, like wild colts too long con-fined, and run scream-ing
mf – marc.
De-light-ed chil-dren burst in-to the
scream-ing, dodg-ing flail - ing sheets on new - ly hung clothes - lines. de -
f
mf

979-0-051-48191-0

979-0-051-48191-0

a tempo
Spring! The sweet breath of Spring has blown a-way win - ter's
Spring! The sweet breath of Spring has blown a-way win - ter's
Spring! The sweet breath of Spring has blown a-way win - ter's
Spring! The sweet breath of Spring has blown a-way win - ter's
a tempo
rallentando e dimin.
crum - bling can - vas. Then
crum - bling can - vas. Then
crum - bling can - vas. Then
crum - bling can - vas. Then
rallentando e dimin.

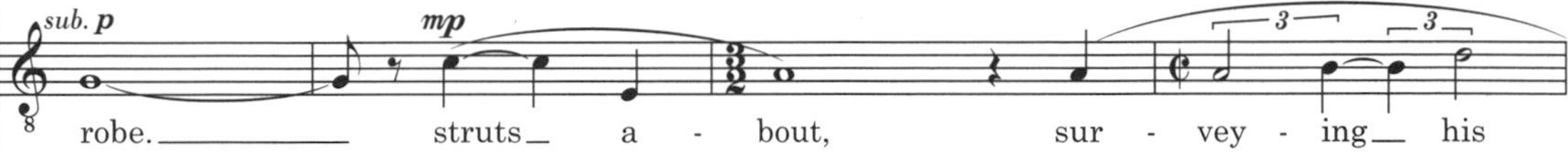

979-0-051-48191-0

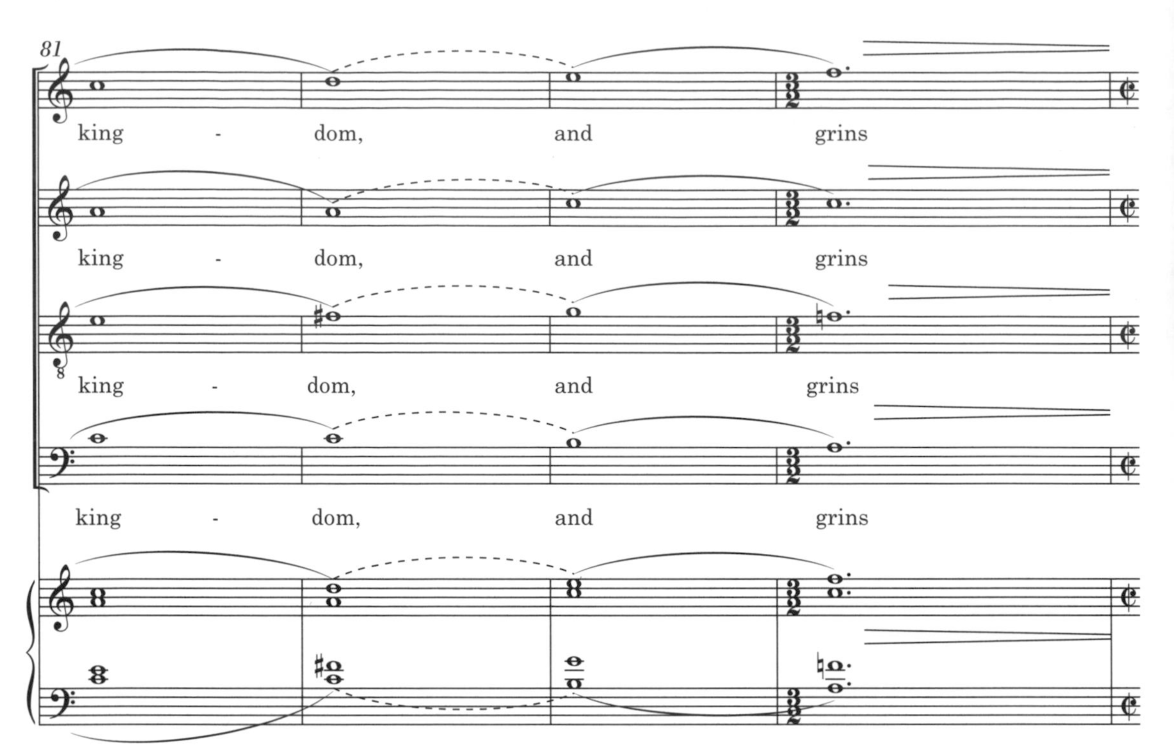
81
king - dom, and grins
king - dom, and grins
king - dom, and grins
king - dom, and grins

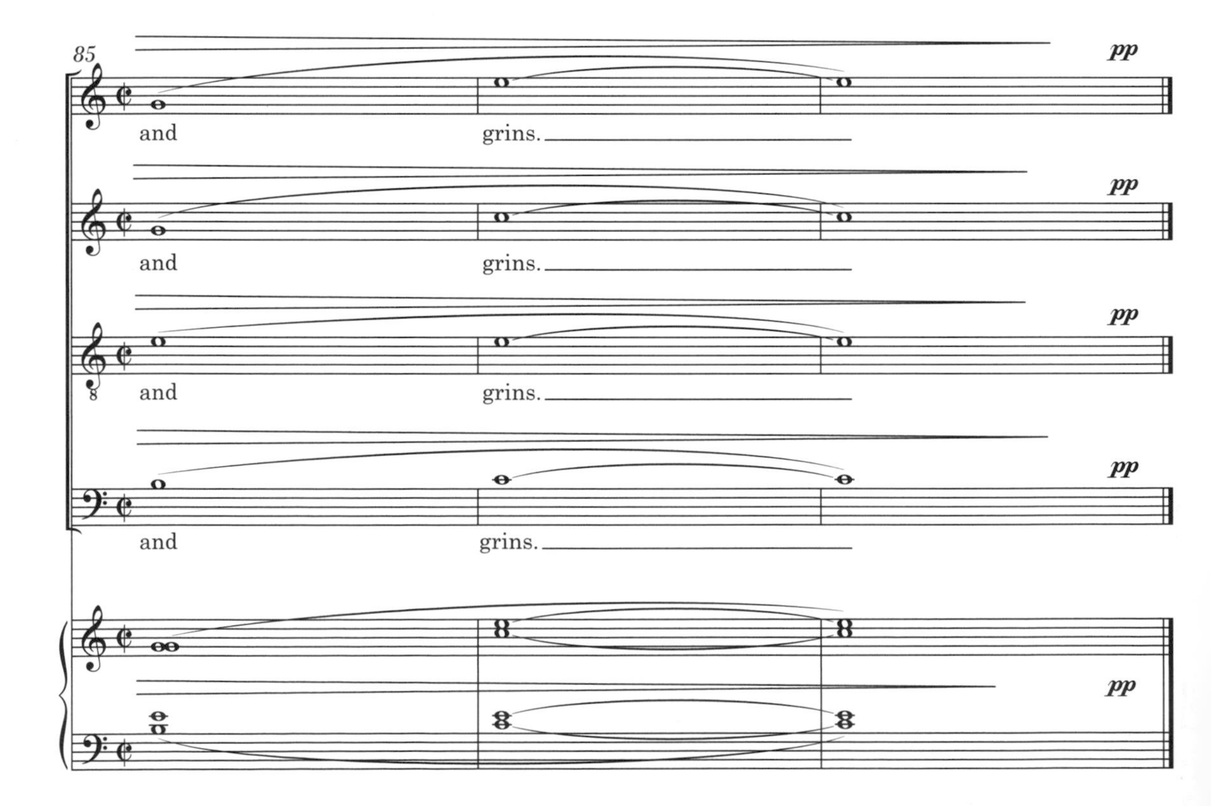
85
and grins.
and grins.
and grins.
and grins.
pp

IV. Summer

Larghetto (♩ = 55)
SOPRANO
ALTO
TENOR
BASS
Out of the mists of Spring, the
Out of the mists of Spring, the God - dess of
Out of the
Out of the mists of
Larghetto (♩ = 55)
PIANO
rehearsal only)
God - dess of Sum - mer ar - rives, arms out - stretched, ea - ger to per-
Sum - mer ar - rives, out of the mists of Spring, arms out - stretched, ea - ger to per-
mists the God - dess ar - rives, arms out - stretched, ea - ger to per-
Spring, the God - dess ar - rives, arms out - stretched, ea - ger to per-

9
mf
-form her an-nu-al mir-a-cle. Her joy-ful ac-o-lytes shed their
14
p - dolce
mp
mf
p
poco a poco cresc.
leaf-y bed-clothes. Ferns un-furl, cor-al bells a-wak-en, ros-es lift their

979-0-051-48191-0

26
poco più f
night skies, in con - cert with
night skies, in con - cert with
night skies, in con - cert with
mp
Fire - flies flick - er in night skies
28
mf
cresc.
moon - light with moon - light
moon - light with moon - light
moon - light with moon - light
poco più f
and in con-cert with moon-light fire - flies flick-er in night skies in

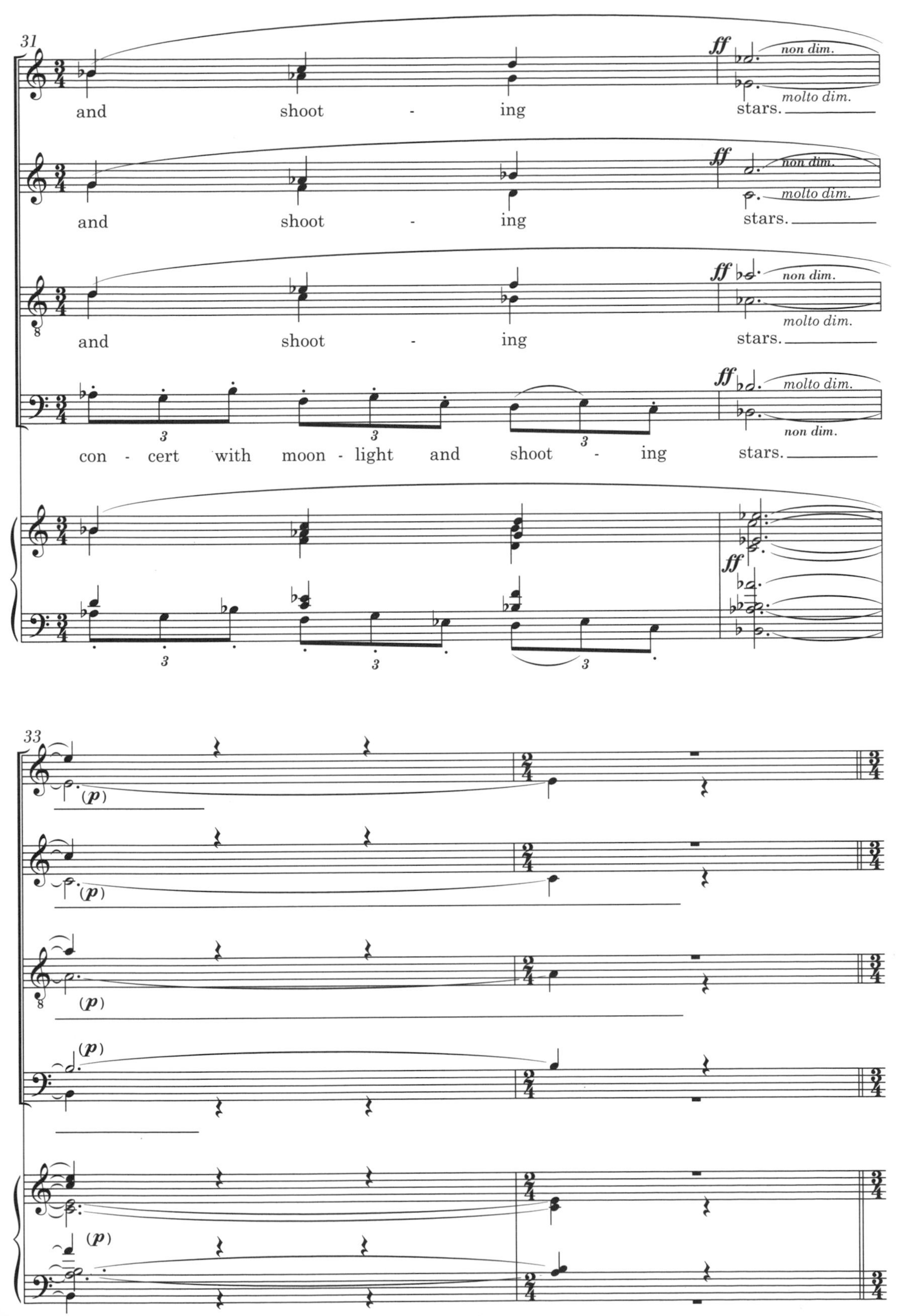
31
ff
non dim.
molto dim.
and shoot - ing stars.
ff
non dim.
molto dim.
and shoot - ing stars.
ff
non dim.
molto dim.
and shoot - ing stars.
ff
molto dim.
non dim.
con - cert with moon - light and shoot - ing stars.
3
ff
33
(p)
(p)
(p)
(p)
(p)

35
mp
mf
mp
mf
Bathed in this ce - les - tial light, fra - grant an - gel's trum - pets
39
con portamento
re - flect a ghost - ly glow.

Stesso tempo ma quasi corale
44
mf
f
Soon, the God-dess of Sum-mer sees that all is pro-ceed-ing as planned.
Soon, the God-dess of Sum-mer sees that all is pro-ceed-ing, pro-ceed-ing as
Soon, the God-dess of Sum-mer sees that all is pro-ceed-ing as planned.
Soon, the God-dess of Sum-mer sees that all is pro-ceed-ing as planned.
Stesso tempo ma quasi corale
51
poco a poco decrescendo
Though re - luc-tant to leave, she nods and sad-ly be - stows her
planned. Re - luc-tant to leave, she nods and sad-ly be - stows her
Though re - luc-tant to leave, she nods and sad-ly be - stows her
Though re - luc-tant to leave, she nods and sad-ly be - stows her

979-0-051-48191-0